Family Violence

"My Parents Hurt Each Other!"

by Kate Havelin

Consultant:
Martha Farrell Erickson, PhD
Director of Children, Youth, and Family Consortium
University of Minnesota

Perspectives on Relationships

LifeMatters
an imprint of Capstone Press
Mankato, Minnesota

LifeMatters books are published by Capstone Press
818 North Willow Street • Mankato, Minnesota 56001
http://www.capstone-press.com

Printed in the United States of America

Library of Congress Cataloging-in-Publication Data
Havelin, Kate, 1961–
     Family violence: my parents hurt each other! / by Kate Havelin.
         p. cm. — (Perspectives on Relationships)
     Includes bibliographical references and index.
     Summary: Describes spousal and child abuse with emphasis on its possible causes and what people have done and can do to stop it.
     ISBN 0-7368-0286-X (book). — ISBN 0-7368-0295-9 (series)
     1. Family violence Juvenile literature. 2. Child abuse Juvenile literature. [1. Family violence. 2. Child abuse.] I. Title.
     II. Series.
     HV6626.H326 2000
     362.82′92—dc21   99-31164
                                 CIP

Staff Credits
Kristin Thoennes, editor; Adam Lazar, designer; Kimberly Danger, photo researcher

Photo Credits
Cover: PNI/©RubberBall
International Stock/©Ken Tannenbaum, 11; ©Scott Campbell, 29; ©Noblestock, 53; ©Michael Philip Manheim, 27, 30
©PhotoDisc, Inc./Everyday People, 36, 59
Ranibow/©Frank Sitemann, 31; ©Tom McCarthy, 6
©Rubberball Productions/ Faces Volume One, 17, 58
©James L. Shaffer, 34, 39, 42, 47
Transparencies/©Tom McCarthy, 9
Unicorn Stock Photos/©D&I MacDonald, 24; ©Deneve Feigh Bunde, 22; ©Martin R. Jones, 19; ©Jeff Greenberg, 45; ©Eric Berndt, 54; ©Dennis MacDonald, 51
Visuals Unlimited/©Jeff Greenberg, 15

A 0 9 8 7 6 5 4 3 2 1

Table of Contents

Chapter Overview

Family violence is very common. Many children live with people who hurt others in the family.

Family violence can happen to anyone—rich or poor, young or old, male or female. Most victims of domestic violence, however, are women.

The three main types of family violence are physical, sexual, and emotional.

Family violence often follows a three-step cycle of building tension, violence, and guilt.

Chapter 1

What Is Family Violence?

Lisa's Dad Is Mad Again

He came home from work in a bad mood. The family knows to be quiet when Dad is angry. Lisa and her sister Beth went right to their rooms after dinner. They heard their parents arguing.

Sometimes Lisa thinks that all her parents do is fight. Tonight, though, the fighting seems worse. Lisa and Beth hear screams and dishes slamming on the floor. The sisters are scared but don't know what to do. They hear slapping sounds followed by more yelling and crying. The door slams.

The girls run downstairs to find their mom on the floor. She is bruised and crying. Again.

Abuse Happens in Many Homes

Home can be a scary place for many families. Home is where some moms, dads, kids, and step-parents hurt each other. It is frightening to live in a violent home. Many children see their parents hitting or being hit. Every 15 to 18 seconds, somebody is hit by a loved one.

This kind of violence has different names. Some people call it domestic abuse or domestic violence. Others say it is wife beating, spousal abuse, or battering. Regardless of what it's called, violence is a crime. It is against the law to seriously hurt other people in one's family or household. It is also against the law to threaten them.

Sometimes the violence occurs between a married couple. Sometimes it occurs between people who live together or who used to live together. Family violence usually refers to problems between people who have a serious relationship. Family violence also includes abuse against children. This book deals mostly with how violence between adults affects children and teenagers.

Family Violence Happens in Different Ways

The most common kind of domestic violence is man against woman. Sometimes women hit men. Sometimes women hit women or men hit men. Ninety-five percent of all domestic violence victims, however, are female. This book sometimes refers to abusers as men and victims as women.

Violence happens when one person tries to control another person. Abusers often use more than one kind of violence to control their partners. The main kinds of family violence are:

Physical

Physical violence is any act meant to injure or hurt another person's body. Examples include:

Hitting
Slapping
Pushing
Grabbing
Burning
Pinching
Choking
Punching
Stabbing
Shooting

Fast Fact

Each day, four to five women are killed in America by their male partners.

Many people think of black eyes and bruises as signs of physical abuse. But not all physical abuse leaves marks. Yanking someone's hair or breast might not leave a mark. It still hurts, however, and it is still physical abuse.

Sexual

Sexual violence includes any sexual act that people are forced to do against their will. This may or may not include intercourse. It can include making someone have sex while others watch.

Emotional

Emotional violence is the hardest to prove. It is also the toughest to overcome. It includes anything that is repeatedly said or done to make another person feel bad. Most people occasionally say unkind words to another person. Emotional abuse, however, refers to a pattern of cruel words or acts. It includes:

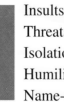

Insults
Threats
Isolation
Humiliation
Name-calling

Emotional abuse can also mean dominating a person by controlling his or her money or social life. The following examples help to illustrate this.

Controlling Others

Tara Tries to "Own" Mark
Tara doesn't want her boyfriend Mark to have any other friends. She is jealous of anyone he likes. She doesn't even want him to visit his family. Tara wants to be the most important person in Mark's life. Mark is frustrated. He likes Tara, but he wants some time alone and time with other friends.

Edward Controls the Money and His Wife
Grace and Edward have been married 15 years. She stays at home to care for their three children while Edward goes to work. Grace does the shopping but has to ask Edward for money. He refuses to let Grace get a job. Edward thinks he is in charge because he controls the household money.

About half of all homeless women and children are trying to escape domestic violence.

The Three-Step Violence Cycle

Family violence often follows a three-step cycle.

First: TENSION

The abuser gets mad but can usually be calmed down. Fights may happen, but they are verbal, not physical. The abused person may try to ignore warning signs that things are getting worse.

Second: VIOLENCE

The abuser becomes violent, hitting and sometimes causing severe injuries.

Third: GUILT

The abuser feels sorry for what has happened. Abusers often try to apologize to their victims. They give gifts and promise the violence will never happen again. These promises make the victim feel loved and valued. At those moments, it is easy to believe the abuser's promises. However, the cycle often continues. More than 1,500 American women are killed by their current or former husbands or partners every year. One in ten women in Canada is assaulted by her partner.

Points to Consider

What do people in your family do when they get mad?

What excuses might an adult who is abused make for the abuse?

Are you afraid of someone in your family? If so, why?

What are some other examples of emotional abuse?

How do you think emotional abuse makes a person feel?

Chapter Overview

Family violence hurts everyone in a family, even those who aren't abused.

Children who grow up in violent families are likely to be abused themselves. Parents who abuse each other are more likely to abuse their kids.

Violence is a learned behavior. Kids who see their parents use violence to solve problems are more likely to use violence themselves.

Boys and girls who grow up with abuse get different messages about it. Boys may become more physical and aggressive. Girls may become more passive and withdrawn.

Chapter 2

How Family Violence Hurts Kids

Everyone who lives in a violent home suffers. Family violence is not healthy for men, women, or children. Home should feel like a safe place to be. Families should protect kids from dangers. Instead, what happens inside the family hurts some kids.

Children whose parents hit one another often feel shame, guilt, and fear. The kids are sometimes afraid they will be hurt. They may be afraid of what one parent will do to the other. They often are angry, depressed, and tense and often have nightmares.

Children in these families may blame themselves. They sometimes think that if they were better kids, their parents wouldn't fight. This is especially true when parents are fighting about the children.

Most kids who grow up with abuse think they have a shameful secret. Those kids are not alone. More than three million American children witness family violence each year.

Mara Avoids Friends

Mara has grown up watching her parents fight. It scares her. Sometimes it makes her mad. She doesn't want people to know her parents hit each other. Mara never invites friends to her house.

Recently a boy in Mara's English class had been paying attention to her. Luis often talked to her by her locker. Last week, he asked Mara if he could walk her home. She said no and quickly turned away. She did not want him to meet her family. Now Luis thinks Mara does not like him. Her parents' violence is a secret Mara is ashamed to share.

Violence Between Parents Hurts Kids

The abuser may never hit the children, but the children still suffer. Family violence destroys kids' sense of safety. It robs their self-confidence. It warps their sense of family and shapes the way they think about love. The stress of living with abuse also makes it hard to focus on school.

Children who live with domestic abuse may show some signs of stress. Those signs include some or all of the following:

Problems sleeping or eating

Problems with school (refusal to go, truancy, poor grades)

Clinging to parent or siblings

Tendency to kick, hit, or fight

Overreaction to discipline

Acting as if they are the parent

Stealing

Lying

Headaches, ulcers, rashes

Hearing and speech problems

Some kids drop out or run away to escape the abuse. Teens in abusive homes are more likely to run away or try suicide. Children who live with violence are 50 percent more likely to abuse alcohol and other drugs than those who don't live with violence.

One-half to three-fourths of men who abuse their wives or girlfriends also abuse the kids in the home.

Children who live with abusive parents are likely to be hit themselves. A person who cannot handle anger is likely to use violence to solve problems. Battered mothers are more likely than other mothers to abuse their kids.

Kids Often Repeat Parents' Mistakes

Young people who grow up seeing abuse often repeat the cycle. Kids whose parents yell and hit often do the same when they are frustrated. Those kids do not learn healthy ways to handle anger. It does not take long for kids to learn bad lessons from watching domestic abuse.

Elementary school kids who see abuse can pick up different messages about family violence. Boys who see their father hitting their mother learn that it's okay to hit women. Girls who see their mother being hit learn that women should accept abuse.

Boys who grow up with abuse are more likely to:

Become aggressive

Have problems controlling their temper

Be disruptive in class

Girls who grow up with abuse are more likely to:

Be withdrawn

Become passive

Cling to other people

Act dependent

Family violence also hurts kids in another way. Kids in abusive homes learn that people who love them will hurt them. That makes it hard for kids to trust anyone. They believe they will be physically or emotionally hurt. Therefore, kids who live with family violence may grow up afraid to get close to other people.

"Children who witness violence, even though they are not abused, learn and repeat what they see at home."
—Judge Diane Dal Santo

Robert Shifts the Blame

Robert cannot remember the first time he saw his father hit his mom. Robert hated his father, blaming him for the fights. Once, when he was eight, Robert tried to punch his dad to make him stop. His dad just knocked him out of the way.

Robert could not understand why his mother stayed with someone who beat her up. Robert began to feel less sorry for his mom. He started to blame her for the family fights. He thought it was his mother's fault that his dad got so mad.

Then one day, Robert's mother yelled at him because his room was messy. Without thinking, Robert pushed her out of his room. When she came back in, he hit her. Robert and his mother just looked at each other. No one said anything. Robert's mom turned and walked away. He heard her crying downstairs. He stood in his room alone. Robert never thought he would grow up to hit someone he loved.

Points to Consider

How do kids learn how to handle problems?

Name three ways you could deal with someone who made you mad.

What would you think if a friend told you his parents hit each other?

Would your friends understand if your parents were abusive?

Why might boys and girls get different messages about abuse?

Chapter Overview

Most abusers grew up seeing violence. They never learned peaceful ways to handle anger.

Abusers want to be in control, but they often are afraid of being abandoned.

Women have not been treated as equals throughout history. Many men believe they have the right to control women.

Alcohol and other drugs do not cause abuse.

Chapter 3

Why Do Abusers Do It?

"It will never happen again. I promise. This time, everything will be different."

Here We Go Again

Judy has heard those words before. Again her dad is promising her mother that he will not hurt her. Last night, Judy's dad got drunk and punched her mother. Today he swears that was the last time. Her dad is probably hugging her mom. He is being gentle, the way he can be when he chooses.

Judy and her family have seen the cycle before. Her dad gets increasingly angry. He drinks more. Finally, he snaps and hits her mom. Then he says he is sorry and buys her gifts. Sometimes it takes months before the next big fight. But it always happens again.

Why do people hit those they love? People hurt other people for many reasons. Experts who study domestic abuse, however, see several clear patterns.

Abusers Do What They Experienced While Growing Up

First, experts say violence is a learned behavior. People who grow up seeing abuse are more likely to become abusers or abused. Boys who witness abuse are three times more likely to abuse their own wives. Boys who grow up seeing extremely violent abuse are 1,000 percent more likely to grow up to abuse than boys from peaceful homes! Therefore, if someone in your home is abusive, that person probably grew up seeing abuse or being abused.

Abusers Want Power

People who batter their partners want to feel in control. They want to be powerful and strong. Usually abusers do not feel good about themselves. They may not feel secure about work, money, or other parts of life. Abusers think that if they can control others, they will be powerful.

Abusers Are Afraid

Abusers are often scared. They are afraid their partner will leave them. They do not want the other person to have this power. So the abusers hit the people they love in order to control them. This is evident from the following fact: Husbands are five times more likely to kill their wife during separation than before or after a divorce.

Abusers Think They Have the Right

Throughout history, men have considered women to be second class citizens. Women were not considered equal to men. Instead, men thought of women as a kind of property—something to own. Many countries had laws giving men great power over women. For example:

Men in Ancient Rome were allowed to divorce or kill a wife who got drunk in public.

Women in the European Middle Ages were beaten or burned alive for threatening their husband.

Women in Colonial America had no legal rights, and husbands were permitted to beat their wife.

Even now, our society sends confusing messages about women's rights. Many TV shows, movies, songs, and ads show women as sex objects. Some boys and men consider women as *things* to be controlled.

Jon and Julie have been married for 17 years. Their sons Tim and Mark have **Jon "Loves" Julie** grown up seeing Jon hit Julie. Jon is certain he has never really hurt his wife. He just wants her to know that he is in charge. Jon expects Julie to obey him.

Jon grew up seeing his own dad dominate his mother. When Jon was 16, his mother left home. Eventually his parents divorced. Jon does not want that to happen to him. Therefore, he tries to control Julie.

Sometimes Julie makes him mad. She will not listen to him. Jon thinks Julie does not respect him. That's when he hits her. He tells himself he loves her. He just doesn't want her to leave.

Alcohol and Other Drugs Do Not Cause Abuse

Many people think domestic abuse happens because someone drank too much. That is a myth. Under the influence of alcohol and other drugs, people may feel more free to act out. Alcohol and other drugs are not, however, the cause of the abuse. The violence happens because the abuser chooses to abuse. Abusers with severe alcohol problems are just as likely to abuse when they are sober. They are more likely to harm someone seriously when they are drunk.

Some abusers explain their behavior by saying things that are not true. For example, abusers may say:
"I just wanted her to listen."
"I only pushed her."
"It's her fault. She made me do it."

Experts say 8 to 30 percent of batterers also abuse drugs. Some drugs like amphetamines and PCP (angel dust) are more likely to cause people to become violent. Those drugs give people more energy and keep them awake. Too much energy and too little sleep can make it hard to think clearly.

Another myth is that abusers lose control and cannot stop themselves. The fact is that people can decide how to behave. They can choose to hit others, or they can choose to handle problems in other ways. For example, they can choose to leave or to talk.

Points to Consider

Do you think domestic abuse has happened among earlier generations of your family? Why or why not?

What kind of messages did your grandparents send your parents about violence?

How has history's view of women affected people today?

Can you think of songs or movies that treat women as things to be owned or controlled?

Why are alcohol and other drugs often blamed for abuse?

Chapter Overview

Women who are abused may stay with their abusers for many reasons.

Continued abuse hurts a person's sense of self. Low self-esteem, guilt, and blaming oneself are common reactions to repeated abuse.

Battered woman syndrome affects some people who are often abused. They may think they cannot stop the abuse and that no one can help them.

People who are abused are more likely to abuse alcohol or other drugs. Battered women are also more likely to attempt suicide.

Why Do Some Women Stay?

Feeling Stuck With the Violence

Bruises. Blood. One sprained wrist. Two broken ribs. Leah can list everything that Marcus, her live-in boyfriend, has done to her. They've been together three years. Marcus treats her okay except when he gets high and loses his temper. Leah wishes he would stop doing drugs. But sometimes she gets high with him.

Lately Leah has been drinking to forget the fights. She swears she will leave Marcus if he hurts her seven-year-old son, Tony. She wants things to be better. She remembers how happy she and Marcus used to be. Now she and Tony are both scared. Leah does not know how to make things better.

Four million incidents of domestic abuse are reported each year. The National Coalition Against Domestic Violence estimates that up to 90 percent of abused women never report the abuse.

Sometimes it is hard to understand why a woman stays with someone who hurts her. Many people believe that only a certain kind of woman gets abused. This is not true. All kinds of women—young, old, rich, poor, educated or uneducated—are battered. Domestic abuse happens to people of all racial, ethnic, and religious groups.

Too often people blame women for not leaving their abusers. It can be very hard for a woman to leave. Experts say women stay in abusive relationships for many reasons.

Victims Are Shaped by Their Childhood

There is no clear evidence that girls who grow up seeing domestic abuse are more likely to be abused as adults. There is evidence, however, that many abused women grow up in families that believe women should obey men. As girls, these women saw their mothers treated poorly. The girls learned to associate love and hurt. Therefore, they may have grown up feeling that hurtful attention is better than none at all.

Victims Need Their Homes, Kids, and Money

Sometimes women think they cannot afford to leave a bad situation. People who are repeatedly abused often:

Have nowhere else to live

Depend on their abusers for money for themselves and their kids

Want their kids to be with their father

Still love the abuser

Are part of a religion or culture that disapproves of women leaving their husband

Victims Face Danger if They Leave

The most dangerous time for an abused woman is when she decides to leave her abuser. Some abusers threaten death if the woman tries to leave. Sometimes abusers threaten to hurt their children if women leave. One study found that half of all domestic murders happen after couples separate or divorce.

Victims Do Not Believe Anything Can Change

People who are repeatedly hit, threatened, or humiliated often lose hope. They stop trusting themselves. They do not feel strong and able to escape the abuse. They become helpless and blame themselves for the abuse.

People who work with abuse victims sometimes call that hopelessness battered woman syndrome. This syndrome is a pattern of behaviors common to many people who are abused.

What Happens to Victims Over Time?

People who are repeatedly abused often share these characteristics. They may:

- Have low self-esteem
- Blame themselves for the abuse
- Feel helpless to stop the abuse
- Feel angry and scared at the same time
- Tend to deny the situation
- Become depressed

It is important to note that abuse does not happen because a person has low self-esteem. Repeated abuse hurts a person's body and spirit. The low self-esteem and hopelessness usually occur because of the abuse. One study of almost 500 battered women found that they are 8 times more likely than other women to attempt suicide.

Alcohol and Other Drugs May Deter Women From Leaving

People who are abused sometimes turn to alcohol and other drugs to dull their pain. One study found that battered women are 15 times more likely than other women to abuse alcohol. That same study showed that abused women are six times more likely to abuse drugs than women who are not abused.

Alcohol and other drugs may temporarily block pain. They can, however, put victims in more danger. People who are drunk or high are less able to anticipate and respond to crises.

I am scared about my **Kim Worries About Her Mom** mother. Her boyfriend Sam has been hitting her again. He calls her names and says she is stupid. I think mom is starting to believe what Sam says.

Mom used to be fun to be around. Now she always puts herself down. She has few friends left. Sam doesn't want mom to spend time with her old crowd. Lately mom is already drunk when I come home from school. The last time Sam got mad, she was too drunk to see it coming. I think she got drunk on purpose.

I want to help my mom, but she pretends everything is okay. I know things are bad. But I do not know how to make my mom see that. We used to talk about everything. Now, I feel alone and scared.

Points to Consider

Why do some people stay with their abusers?

How would you feel if someone always called you names or hurt your feelings?

Do you think being hit or hurt repeatedly would change how you feel about yourself?

Why is having high self-esteem important?

Children who live with family violence often feel lost. Even young people have some power, however. You can choose how to act. You can work to be safe. But you cannot stop the violence! The only person who can stop abuse is the abuser.

Young people are not responsible for the violence. You cannot break the cycle of violence. Kids who try to stop fights between parents risk getting hurt themselves. One study reports that 62 percent of teenaged sons who try to intervene are injured.

You Can Ask for Help

You can do something to change the situation. One of the most important steps you can take is to tell someone about the abuse. Family violence is a secret nobody should keep. You can take some of the abuser's power away by telling his or her secret. Kids cannot solve the problem alone. They need to tell someone who can help.

Teachers, counselors, and other professionals can help you. They have to report the family violence to police or other authorities. It probably feels scary to think of the police talking to your parents. Just remember that the police are there to help your family.

Neighbors and friends also may be able to help. They can listen to your story. They can offer you a safe place to go if you need to escape from home.

Be careful where you keep this book. Some abusers may become angry if they see someone trying to stop the abuse. Consider hiding it in a backpack or at a friend's house.
—Mick, age 15

Make a Personal Safety Plan

You can make a personal safety plan. That means you can do these things:

Find an adult in your neighborhood or at school whom you can trust.

Tell that trusted person about the abuse.

Use a code word with that person when abuse happens.

Call 911 when necessary.

Paul Makes a Plan

Paul was worried about the violence in his family. He realized he could not stop the fights. But someone had to do something. Paul told his basketball coach about his parents' fights. The coach listened and steered Paul to Anne, the school counselor. Anne helped Paul make a safety plan.

Paul's parents still fight, but Paul feels a little safer. He still talks to Anne. Together they made a list of things Paul could do when his parents fight. Paul knows if the fight turns serious, he can call Anne and say their code word. She agreed to call the police if that happens.

Paul's Safety Plan

1 **Practice ways to get out of your home during a fight.**
Paul knows he can jump out a first-floor window when his parents become violent.

2 **Be ready to flee.**
Paul keeps some clothes, his school ID, his keys, and some money in his backpack. He also has included some medicine for his asthma. The backpack is ready if he needs to leave in a hurry.

3 **Set up a safe place to go.**
Paul knows he can always stay at his friend Ralph's place. Ralph's family lives three blocks away, so Paul can easily get there. It felt scary to tell Ralph why he might need a place to stay. However, Ralph listened with understanding. Paul feels better now that a friend knows.

4 **Make a code word.**
Paul can call Anne or Ralph when his parents lose control. Anne and Ralph know that if Paul says tornado, he needs help. They will call the police to protect Paul.

If you are being abused, you must try to protect yourself:

- Protect your face, chest, and abdomen if you are being attacked.

- Ask medical staff to photograph your injuries. The pictures can prove to a judge that you were hurt.

- Save any items the abuser ripped, cut, or broke. They are evidence of the violence in your home.

You Can Become More Independent

Another way to protect yourself is to become more independent. You may want to learn the public transit system. That way, you can get to school, work, and appointments on your own. Consider getting a part-time job so that you have some money. You might want to open a bank account in your own name to begin saving money. Eventually you will be old enough to move out of your home.

Until then, however, it is very important to protect yourself. Your goal is to be safe. You cannot reason with angry abusers. They will not listen. Do not try to hit an abuser to stop the attacks. You likely will be hit in return.

Medical bills for victims of domestic abuse reach $3 to $5 billion a year in the United States.

Family violence is frightening. It is more than kids can handle alone. The *Community Services* section of the phone book lists many groups who can help you.

If you don't feel comfortable with that, consider talking to some of these people:

- Relatives
- Neighbors
- Teachers
- Coaches
- Doctors
- Counselors
- Women's shelter advocates
- Police officers

Points to Consider

How would you get out of your house if your parents were fighting?

Can you think of someone you would trust to tell about family violence?

How does becoming more independent help teens who live with abuse?

What would you say if a friend told you his or her parents were violent?

Chapter Overview

Families usually cannot stop the violence by themselves. People outside the family such as advocates can help stop the cycle of violence.

Advocates are trained to help people who have been abused. They know what is safe and what is dangerous for abused families.

Shelters offer a safe place for women and children who have been abused.

Advocates can help abuse survivors understand why abuse happens and what will stop it.

Advocates also can help abuse survivors regain self-esteem and build a new life.

Chapter 6

Advocates Can Help Break the Cycle

Carla Calls the Police

Carla's parents were hitting each other again. When her mother reached for a knife, Carla called 911. Within minutes, two police officers came to the door.

The officers tried to talk with Carla's parents. But her mom and dad were so angry that they just kept trying to hit each other. Each officer pinned one parent. The police took both parents to the police station in handcuffs.

Carla went to stay at a neighbor's. She felt sad and scared to see her parents taken away. However, she knew that calling the police may have saved her parents' lives.

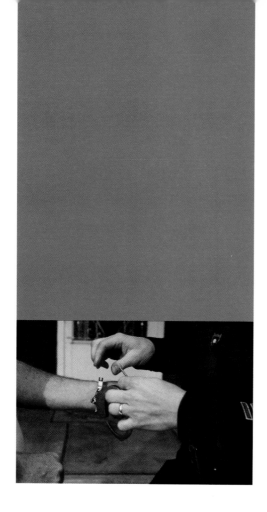

Family violence rarely stops by itself. It is difficult for a family to break that cycle alone. Usually someone else needs to step in and help. Many people such as police and women's advocates are trained to help violent families.

Police can break up a fight. Sometimes they can calm parents down. They can arrest a suspected abuser. But police cannot prevent the violence from happening next time.

Family Violence

The United States has more than 2,500 shelters, hotlines, and safe home networks.

Advocates Work to Make Women and Children Safe

Women's advocates assist people who have been abused. The advocates often work in shelters. Shelters are safe places designed for women and their children who are fleeing domestic violence. Shelters usually look like ordinary houses or buildings, but they have extra security. They often are full of women and kids who have escaped dangerous situations.

Advocates listen and give advice to women and young people. Advocates can help victims make educated choices about their lives. They may help an abused person realize she needs to leave her abusive partner. They can help people find apartments or jobs to begin a new, safer life. Advocates know how to help people deal with the pain and shame of family abuse.

Myth: Domestic abuse is a private family matter. People outside a family should stay out of the family's private life.

Fact: Domestic abuse is a crime. It needs to be stopped and punished. Police and advocates step in when violence happens.

Joe Goes to a Shelter

"Bzzzzzzzzz!" The doorbell outside the women's shelter buzzes loudly. Thirteen-year-old Joe, his sisters, and their mom are all nervous, so the noise scares them. Everything scares them. Joe's mom called the shelter after his dad went to work. Joe's dad was becoming more and more violent. They had to leave home.

A gentle-looking woman opens the shelter door and brings them inside. No one in Joe's family has ever been to a shelter before. From the outside, it looks like any other house on the block. But the front door is sturdy and doesn't have any glass. The only way to get in is by buzzing and stating who you are. A security camera lets the shelter workers see visitors before opening the door.

Once inside, Joe and his family see a large living room. There are couches and a big TV. Some kids are on the floor doing puzzles. Liz is the shelter advocate who greeted them. She takes them to a room where they can sleep and keep their things.

Liz shows them around the whole shelter and explains the routine. Everyone who stays at the shelter has some chores and responsibilities. No one is allowed to hit another person at a shelter. Alcohol and drugs are forbidden. And everyone takes part in some kind of support group.

Liz explains that support groups help women and kids deal with their abuse. The groups help families understand why abuse happens. Then families can work to break those patterns and begin healing.

Little kids like Joe's seven-year-old sister draw pictures to show how they feel. The teens in Joe's support group put on skits about their thoughts and emotions. Joe's mom meets with a small group of other abused women. Each group meets several times a week. Joe's mom also talks with counselors about finding work.

Liz said Joe and his family were welcome to stay at the shelter for several weeks. For now, this would be Joe's home. The shelter doesn't look like their home, but Joe feels safe. It has been a long time since he has felt safe.

Martha McWhirter opened the first women's shelter in 1875 in Belton, Texas.

Advocates help people rebuild their self-esteem. Shelter workers can help families to stop feeling like victims. Instead, those families can begin to feel like survivors of abuse. It takes time for families to feel safe and strong again. Many families, however, do overcome the abuse.

Advocates Can Explain How Courts Work

Advocates can help victims of domestic violence another way. Domestic abuse is a crime that should be punished. The laws and courts can be confusing to people who are not lawyers. Advocates understand how courts work. Advocates can help families go through the process of getting justice.

Help From City Governments

Some cities require police to arrest suspected abusers even when victims refuse to press charges. Duluth, Minnesota, and San Diego, California, were the first cities to try mandatory arrest. Domestic abuse rates dropped after police began arresting all suspected abusers. Until then, police often let suspects stay in their homes. Now dozens of states have mandatory arrest laws.

Points to Consider

Would you ever call the police to break up a family fight? How would you feel? How would your parents react?

What kind of services do you think a shelter needs to help women and children?

Does your community have any shelters? Check the phone book under *Crisis Intervention Services* or *Women's Organizations* for shelters.

How would you feel if you went to a shelter?

Chapter Overview

Judges can help people who have been abused.

Courts help abuse victims in three main ways: divorce or separation, civil orders of protection, and/or criminal prosecution of abusers.

Laws have become tougher against abusers. States must enforce each other's protection orders.

The National Domestic Violence Hotline can help steer people to local shelters and programs.

Chapter 7

Courts Help Abused Adults and Kids

The justice system is set up to protect people's rights. Everyone has the right to be protected against abuse. Family violence is a crime. Judges and others in the court system can help abused people and their families.

One of the earliest legal victories for victims came from an Alabama court in 1871. That court ruled that husbands did not have the right to physically abuse their wives. The ruling said, "A married woman is as much under the protection of the law as any other member of the community."

A Victory for Victims

Courts used to ignore domestic abuse. They thought that what happened in families was private. In 1983, police watched while a woman's husband attacked her. Tracy Thurman was stabbed 13 times while the police did nothing to stop her husband. Later, Thurman sued the city government. She won $2 million from the city of Torrington, Connecticut. However, she remains scarred and partly paralyzed.

Now more judges, police, and prosecutors work to stop abuse. It is not a family matter. Lawmakers have written tougher laws to stop abusers since the women's movement grew in the 1970s. Courts enforce those laws and punish abusers who ignore them.

How Courts Handle Family Violence

Courts usually help families handle violence in one or more of the following ways:

1. Divorce or Separation

Often the only way to stop abuse is to end the relationship between abuser and victim. A battered spouse may decide to divorce or separate from her partner. Divorce means formally ending a marriage. Separation happens when a husband and wife decide to live apart. Judges decide issues concerning a couple's children, money, and property.

2. Civil Order of Protection

An order of protection requires abusers to stay a certain distance away from the abused. Judges issue these orders at the request of the victims. Abusers who disobey protection orders can be arrested, fined, or jailed.

Protection orders can cover:

Whether the abuser will be forced to leave the family home, even if the abuser owns the home

Who will get custody of the children

When and where child visitation happens

Who pays for the victim's moving, medical, and legal costs

Whether the abuser needs treatment or counseling

It is important that victims always carry their protection orders with them. The orders are proof that the abuser is dangerous. Civil protection orders are available in all 50 states and in the District of Columbia. Women's advocates can help victims get protection orders from a civil court judge.

3. Criminal Prosecution of Batterer

Domestic abuse is against the law everywhere in the United States and Canada. Abusers can face penalties in criminal court. They can be arrested, fined, or jailed. Laws about domestic violence vary from state to state. Even so, advocates can help victims and their families get justice.

Tyra's Mom Goes to Court

Today I went to court with my mother. Betsy, the advocate at the shelter where we live, went with us. Mom and Betsy did paperwork before going to court. The papers asked the judge to keep Mom's ex-boyfriend, Robert, away from her.

The judge gave Mom an order of protection. That means Robert will break the law if he goes near Mom. Robert will get a copy of the order so he will know what the judge said. The order is good for six months. Betsy says that will give Mom time to start a new life. Luckily Mom can get another order later if she needs one.

Mom and I worry that Robert will ignore the order. Betsy warned us that abusers sometimes ignore the orders and refuse to stop. Betsy told us to be careful. Mom has to make copies of her order. Police stations near the shelter, Mom's job, and my school should all have copies. That way officers can respond quickly if Robert attacks Mom.

Going to court scared me. But Mom and I feel a little safer now. We know we are doing the right things to stop Robert's violence.

A 1994 Law Helps Protect Women

One of the most important U.S. laws protecting abused people is the Violence Against Women Act of 1994. The law:

- Makes it a federal crime for abusers to cross state lines to hurt their partner

- Forbids some batterers who have been served with a protection order from having guns

- Provides money for programs and services, including the National Domestic Violence Hotline

One Phone Number Links 50 States

The National Domestic Violence Hotline connects people with resources in their community. The national hotline is answered 24 hours a day. Advocates speak English and Spanish and have access to translators who speak 139 languages. The National Domestic Violence Hotline phone number is 1-800-799-SAFE. Telephone numbers that begin with 1-800 are free.

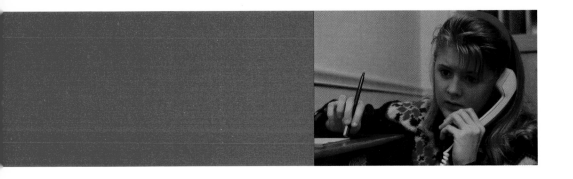

Meredith Makes the Call

"Hello. National Domestic Violence Hotline. This is Candice. Can I help you?"

"Um, I hope so. I, uh, this is hard to say . . . ."

"It's OK. Take your time. Are you or someone you know being abused?"

"Yes, my parents hit each other a lot. I don't know what to do."

"What is your first name? Where do you live?"

"My name is Meredith, and I live in Philadelphia."

"Okay, Meredith, I want to give you the phone numbers of some people there who can help you. Tell me more about what is happening in your family. We can help you, okay?"

"Okay, yes—I was hoping you would be able to help me. I just didn't know who I could tell."

Every U.S. state has some kind of law to prevent abusers from stalking, or repeatedly following, their victims.

Fast Fact

Safe Places for Kids

More than half of the child abductions in the United States occur in families experiencing domestic violence. Forty children are abducted by a parent each hour in the United States. Because of this, the government has created safe places for these kids.

More and more communities are creating supervised visitation centers. The centers are a safe place for children to visit with abusive or violent parents. Two states, New Jersey and Arizona, require such centers.

Points to Consider

Can going to court help families overcome abuse?

Why do courts take abuse more seriously now than they did 30 years ago?

Who would you turn to if your family needed an order of protection?

Should abusers be barred from having guns? Why or why not?

Why might it be hard to call the National Domestic Violence Hotline for help?

Chapter Overview

You are not responsible for the violence.

Family violence is a crime.

You need to try to protect yourself.

Other people can help you.

You can decide not to continue the cycle of violence.

Chapter 8

Important Stuff to Remember

Many parents fight. Some parents hurt each other. Some parents even kill each other. But kids need to remember some important points:

1. You are not responsible for the violence.

Children, including teenagers, cannot control their parents' behavior. Parents need to learn to control themselves. Everyone gets frustrated and upset sometimes. Mature people learn to cope with their anger. Unfortunately some people never learn how to handle stress peacefully. Some parents may not know how to solve problems without violence.

You are not to blame if your parent or parents become violent. Abusers are the only people who are responsible for the abuse. No one wants to be hurt. And no one, especially a child, deserves to be hurt.

2. Family violence is a crime.
It is against the law to attack people in one's family. You can take away some of the abuser's power by not keeping the secret. Tell someone you can trust about the abuse.

3. You need to try to protect yourself.
You cannot stop your parents' abuse, but you can help yourself. Make a personal safety plan to use if a parent tries to hurt you.

4. Other people can help you.
Many people are experienced at helping families overcome violence. School counselors, religious leaders, police, and shelter advocates are among the people in whom you can confide.

You can find someone to talk to about domestic abuse. Check the *Useful Addresses and Internet Sites* section of this book for names of helpful groups. The phone book lists psychologists, shelters, and advocates who can listen and offer guidance.

5. You can decide to not continue the cycle.

Children, especially boys, who live in abusive homes are more likely to become abusers. Many children who witness family violence do not learn healthy ways to cope with anger. You cannot control who your parents are or what they do. You can, however, choose to control yourself.

You can decide to break the cycle of abuse. You can learn to deal with your anger. You can learn to talk about problems instead of hitting someone. You can choose to respect the people you love.

Points to Consider

Prepare a personal safety plan that feels realistic to you.

Name three people you could call if you need help.

Why is it important for you to learn how to deal with anger early in your own life?

How might you get help dealing with anger at this time in your life?

Glossary

abuse (uh-BYOOZ)—to treat a person or creature meanly; it can also mean to treat a thing, like drugs or alcohol, wrongly.

advocate (ad-vuh-KIT)—a person who supports people in trouble; a women's advocate works to help women who have been abused.

batterer (BAT-ur-ur)—a person who repeatedly injures another person

court (KORT)—a place where legal cases are heard and decided

crime (KRIME)—any action that is against the law; it is a crime to abuse another person.

domestic (duh-MESS-tik)—about things that happen in, or are about, home; domestic abuse is violence that happens within a family or a group of people who live together.

emotional (I-MOH-shuh-nuhl)—about feelings; emotional abuse happens when one person repeatedly insults or threatens another person.

guilt (gilt)—a feeling of shame about doing something wrong

order of protection (OR-dur UHV pro-TEK-shun)—an order given by a judge that requires an abuser to stay away from a victim of abuse

physical (FIZ-uh-kuhl)—about the body; physical abuse is any kind of action such as hitting, kicking, slapping, or stabbing that is meant to hurt a person's body.

self-esteem (SELF ess-TEEM)—a feeling of pride and respect for oneself; emotional abuse damages a person's self-esteem.

sexual (SEK-shu-uhl)—about sex; sexual abuse happens when one person forces another to have any kind of sex against his or her will.

shame (SHAYM)—a feeling of guilt or sadness; many children who live with parents who hurt each other feel shame about their family.

shelter (SHEL-tur)—a place where people can go to be safe; a women's shelter is a place where women and their children can go to escape domestic violence.

tension (TEN-shuhn)—a feeling of worry or nervousness; increased tension is the first phase of the cycle of violence.

violence (VEYE-uh-luhnss)—words or actions that hurt people

For More Information

Greenberg, Keith. *Family Abuse: Why Do People Hurt Each Other?* New York: Twenty-First Century Books, 1995.

Havelin, Kate. *Child Abuse: "Why Do My Parents Hit Me?"* Mankato, MN: Capstone Press, 2000.

Havelin, Kate. *Parents: "They're Driving Me Crazy!"* Mankato, MN: Capstone Press, 2000.

Hyde, Margaret. *Know About Abuse.* New York: Walker Publishing Co., 1992.

Kinstlinger-Bruhn, Charlotte. *Breaking the Cycle of Domestic Violence.* New York: Rosen, 1997.

Useful Addresses and Internet Sites

National Coalition Against Domestic Violence
PO Box 18749
Denver, CO 80218

National Center for Victims of Crime
2111 Wilson Boulevard, Suite 300
Arlington, VA 22201

National Clearinghouse on Family Violence
Jeanne Mance Building 1907D1
Tunney's Pasture
Ottawa, ON K1A-1B4
CANADA
1-800-267-1291 (in Canada only)

National Runaway Switchboard
3080 Lincoln Avenue North
Chicago, IL 60657
1-800-621-0394

Access to Justice Network
http://www.acjnet.org/youthfaq/index.html
Provides information to youth on Canadian
law and justice resources

Kids Help Phone
http://www.kidshelp.sympatico.ca/
Provides information to youth who need
information or immediate help with life's
challenges

National Coalition Against Domestic Violence
http://www.ncadv.org/
Offers social change strategies designed to
reduce violence against women and children

Violence Against Women Office
http://www.usdoj.gov.vawo/
Offers statistics, fact sheets, and legislative
updates on violence against women

Index